Ancient Egypt
Treasures, Tombs and Tutankhamen

by
Lorraine Conway

illustrated by Linda Akins

Cover by Janet Skiles

Copyright © Good Apple, Inc., 1987

ISBN No. 0-86653-399-0

Printing No. 9

GOOD APPLE, INC.
BOX 299
CARTHAGE, IL 62321-0299

Ms. Korman

Table of Contents

Time Line for Ancient Egypt

Sixteen important events which took place during ancient Egyptian times are listed below. Use the dates and information to fill in the time line provided for you on the next page. You may wish to add other dates and information as you study ancient Egypt.

3100 B.C.   Egypt was united under Menes who founded the first dynasty.

2700 B.C.   Beginning of the Old Kingdom or Age of the Pyramids.

2100 B.C.   Beginning of the Middle Kingdom or the Age of the Nobles.

1700 B.C.   Egypt is conquered by the Hyskos.

1580 B.C.   Egyptians drive the Hyskos out.

1570 B.C.   Beginning of the New Kingdom.

1500 B.C.   Egyptian Empire reaches its height.

1380 B.C.   Reign of Akhenaten begins. He tries to change the religion of the land to that of one god, Aten, the sun.

1361 B.C.   The reign of Tutankhamen begins. He restores the old gods.

1352 B.C.   Death of Tutankhamen.

1304 B.C.   Reign of Ramses II, great warrior against the Hittites.

1085 B.C.   The Period of Decline begins.

 669 B.C.   Assyrians invade Egypt.

525 B.C.   Persians drive the Assyrians out and take over Egypt.

332 B.C.   Alexander the Great invades Egypt.

 31 B.C.   The army of the last queen of Egypt, Cleopatra, is defeated at Actium. Egypt becomes a province of Rome.

Time Line for Ancient Egypt

3000 B.C.

2000 B.C.

1000 B.C.

Birth of Christ

Introduction

As early as 5000 B.C. small farming villages flourished along the four-thousand-mile-long Nile River. In time these villages banded together to form two countries, Upper and Lower Egypt. Around 3000 B.C. both Egypts were united under King Menes to make the first great Western Civilization. This era of time we refer to as the beginning of Ancient Egypt.

While much of the outside world was inhabited by barbaric tribes, the ancient Egyptians were busy cultivating crops, irrigating the land and building architectural marvels. They devised a system of letters called hieroglyphs and invented a kind of paper making. They also formed an effective government and established trade routes with their neighbors.

Although it was hard, it is certain that these ancient people loved life, for they spent so much time preparing for the one to come. By worshipping a galaxy of gods and goddesses who promised them eternity, meaning and structure was woven into the fabric of their lives.

It is the above aspects in the lives of the ancient Egyptians that this book focuses on. It is hoped that all students who use it will gain a new perspective and lifelong interest in that period of time when the ancient Egyptians were the center of the civilized world.

How the World Began, Egyptian-Style

In the beginning the ancient Egyptians believed that the earth was covered with water and on that great ocean an egg floated. From that egg the sun-god Re, or Ra as he is sometimes referred to, was born. The grandson of Re, Osiris, became the first pharaoh of Egypt and Isis was his queen. They lived happily with their son Horus until Set, the wicked brother of Osiris, became very jealous. In a fit of jealousy, Set murdered his brother and chopped his body into pieces. He took the pieces and scattered them in the Nile River. When Isis found out what happened to her husband, she went about gathering the pieces. She took the pieces to Anubis, the jackal-headed god. Anubis was very clever and he managed to put the pieces together, but he did not have the power to make Osiris human again. From then on Osiris became the god of the dead. His son, Horus, later found Set and slew him for the murder of his father.

From the above story you can easily see that the Egyptians believed that their gods had many human faults as well as superhuman powers. They also had many local gods and sometimes combined two gods into one, as in the case of the sun-god Re, who became Amen-Re. Use the information in the story above to write a short play about "How the World Began, Egyptian-Style," or act it out as a pantomime sketch for your class.

The Nile River, Lifeblood of Egypt

For many reasons the Nile is a strange river. Rising from three great lakes in central Africa, it is known as the White Nile. At Khartoum it is joined by the Blue Nile and becomes simply, the Nile. It continues its 4,000 mile northward flow through deserts, valleys and cataracts of which there are six. At Cairo in Lower Egypt the Nile breaks up into several smaller rivers forming the great fertile delta of Lower Egypt and finally empties into the Mediterranean Sea.

Civilization was born along this great river more than 5,000 years ago. The rich black soil that is deposited as the river yearly floods its banks gives life to the land of Egypt. Without the Nile, Egypt would be a vast desert, for it seldom rains in this part of the world.

QUESTIONS:

1. Trace the path of the White Nile. What three lakes are its source?_____

    _____   _____

2. At what city do the White Nile and the Blue Nile meet? _____

3. For 1,600 miles there are no branches of the Nile. Between which two cities are there no branches? _____

4. As the longest river in the world, it is fortunate that the Nile is navigable for almost its entire length. Boat traffic, however, is impeded by_____, a natural formation.

ACTIVITY:

Using maps and encyclopedias, determine the most important rivers of Europe, Asia, North America and South America. What do each of these rivers have in common with the Nile? How is each different?

The Pyramids

Pyramids were built as burial tombs for ancient Egyptian pharaohs, queens and nobles. The best known pyramids were built during the Old Kingdom about 2664 to 2184 B.C. They were built along the desert away from the Nile River where the land was not suitable for farming. The largest pyramid ever built is that of a pharaoh called Cheops. He was also known as Khufu. Cheop's pyramid is regarded as one of the seven wonders of the ancient world. It has a square base of 756 feet on each side and reaches a height of 450 feet. It is made almost entirely of sandstone rock. The pyramid of Cheops still stands alongside two others near Giza, Egypt.

The base of a pyramid may be square or triangular, but its sides are always triangular. It is thought that as many as 100,000 men using ropes, sledges, levers and ramps worked on and off for about twenty years to build one pyramid. The stones were cut with chisels and axes and came from nearby quarries.

The builders of pyramids did everything possible to keep robbers from stealing the treasures buried with the mummies. Hidden doors, dead end passages and false chambers in most cases only delayed but did not stop tomb robbers. Nobles and pharaohs at the time were enraged at these robberies. Not only were vast treasures taken, leaving the spirit with nothing in the afterlife, but worst of all, if the mummy were destroyed in the robbery, there would be no afterlife.

When the pharaohs finally realized that the pyramids could no longer protect the tombs, they gave up the practice of building them. In 1500 B.C. they began to have their tombs hollowed out of the rocky cliffs that came to be known as the Valley of the Kings. Instead of the large obvious pyramids, small rooms with hidden entrances and rubble piled over the doors became the burial places of later Egyptian pharaohs such as Tutankhamen.

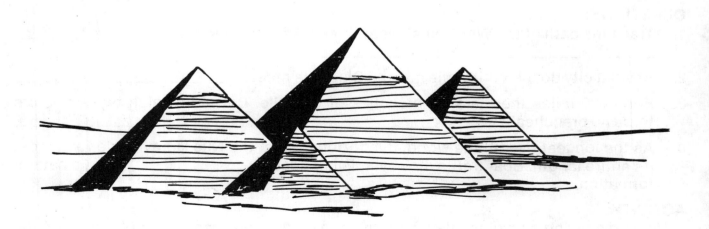

The Seven Wonders of the Ancient World

	THE WONDER	LOCATION	BRIEF DESCRIPTION
1.	Pyramids	Egypt	Built in ancient times as burial tombs for nobility. Cheops is large one.
2.			
3.			
4.			
5.			
6.			
7.			

CHOOSE ONE OF THE FOLLOWING ACTIVITIES:

1. Try making a model of a pyramid. Use cardboard to construct it. Try to make your pyramid to scale using dimensions given in an encyclopedia or other source of information.

2. Thousands of years have passed since the first pyramids were constructed. There have been many inventions and much progress. Think about what is present in the world today. Nominate seven items for the seven wonders of the modern world. Give a reason that you feel each should be included.

3. It is said that up to 100,000 men worked for as long as twenty years to build a pyramid of ancient Egypt. What is something that could be accomplished by the same number of workers in the same length of time today?

Mummification

Egyptian beliefs in life after death led to their complex mummification process. Ancient Egyptians believed that everyone had a soul which they referred to by two names, the ba and the ka. The ba was depicted as a bird with a human head; the ka was the twin of each person. Both the ba and the ka, they believed, were released from the body at the time of death. From then on they did not stay peacefully in one place. Instead the ba returned to live with the family during the day and flew back to the body in its tomb at night. The ka traveled to and from the body to the other world. In order for the ba and the ka to rest in the body at night, it could not be allowed to decay. In other words, the Egyptians believed for the person to live on after death, the body had to be preserved in some way and the best way they knew was that of mummification. After death the bodies of poor and ordinary people were put in the hot dry sand of the desert which preserved them naturally. The bodies of pharaohs and nobles were mummified to further insure preservation, for the Egyptians believed that the pharaohs became gods after death and that their bodies through mummification would last for all eternity.

ACTIVITY:

Research taxidermy. Compare and contrast the process to mummification.

Mummification

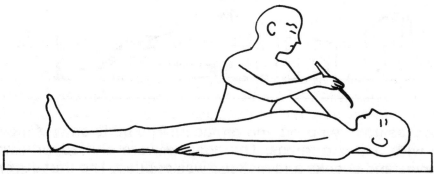

The mummification process began with a ceremony conducted by four priests, with one of the priests dressed as the jackal-headed god, Anubis. The inner organs were removed first as these were the first to decay in the hot climate of Egypt. A special hook was used to remove the brain by working through the nose.

The organs which were taken from the body were placed in special jars called canopic jars. Natron, a special type of salt, was added to the jars for preservation of the organs.

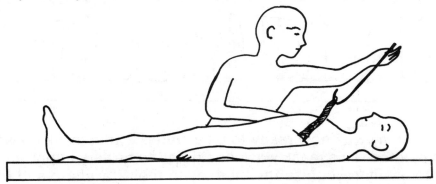

The liver, stomach and intestine were removed by making an incision on the left side of the body. Sometimes the heart was left in the body; sometimes it was removed and replaced by a large carved stone called a scarab.

Linen cloth and natron were used as packing to fill the spaces left when organs were removed.

The body was then ready to be covered with natron and placed on a tilted slab. The natron dried the body of its fluids which drained onto the tilted slab. The body was allowed to dry for at least forty days.

7

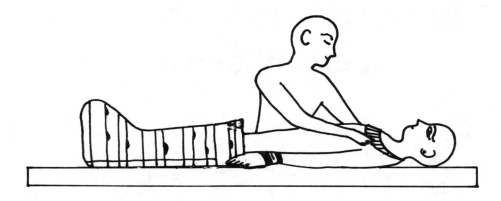

The old packing was now removed and replaced. The incision was sewed up and the body was rubbed with oils and resins. The nostrils were stuffed with wax. Pads were placed under the eyes and cheeks and makeup was applied. The first strips of cloth were wound around the body.

Jewelry was used to decorate the body and good-luck charms were tucked into the twenty or so layers of linen strips which were wound around it. Resins were sometimes used to hold the layers together.

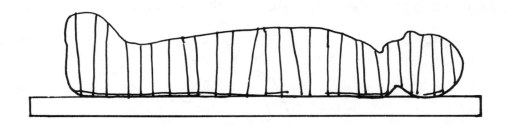

The face of the mummy was now ready to be covered with a mask on which the dead person's face was painted. This mask was considered to be very important as it allowed the ba and the ka to easily recognize the mummy in their travels to and from the body.

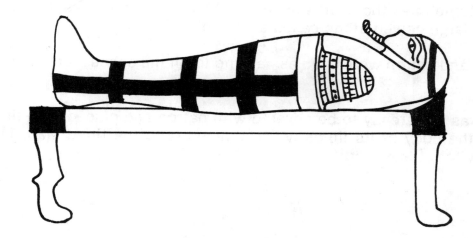

Finally the mummy was placed in a coffin or sometimes a series of coffins one inside the other. It was now ready for the great procession to its final resting place. The whole process of mummification took about seventy days.

A Papier-Mâché Mummy Case

You can easily make a papier-mâché mummy case and do some mummy wrapping if you follow the instructions below.

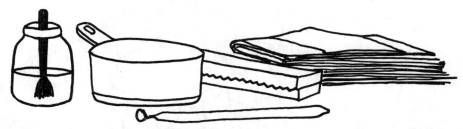

1. Gather the following materials: wheat paste, water, large pan, aluminum wrap or long balloon for frame, newspapers.

2. Make a mixture of the wheat paste and water until the combination is pasty like sour cream.

3. Shape wads of crumpled aluminum foil into a mummy shape or inflate a long balloon. Gently squeeze parts of the balloon to get the shape of a mummy case. Tie the balloon securely.

4. Dip strips of the newspaper into the paste and wrap around the foil or the balloon until you achieve the desired shape.

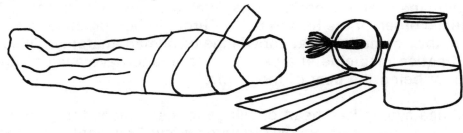

5. Allow the mummy case to dry thoroughly. This may take several days.

6. The case can be sealed by brushing on a coat of undiluted white glue. Sealing is not necessary, but it keeps the colors from running. If you use a sealer, be sure to allow it to dry thoroughly.

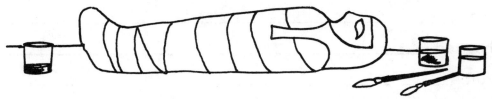

7. Decorate the case Egyptian-style with paints. Draw the traditional portrait mask on the head. When the paints have dried, the mummy case can be glazed with varnish or another commerical glaze. Glazing is not necessary.

VARIATION: Your class may wish to make one life-size mummy case. To do this, make the shape of the mummy from chicken wire. Cover the wire with strips of newspaper dipped into the wheat-paste mixture and wrap around the frame.

The Weighing of the Heart

After the death of a pharaoh and before his soul could enter the afterlife, ancient Egyptians believed that a ceremony called the "weighing of the heart" took place. Presided over by the jackal-headed god, Anubis, and in the presence of the god Osiris and forty-two other gods, the heart of the pharaoh was weighed against the weight of a single feather. If the heart of the pharaoh weighed less than the feather, the pharaoh was declared innocent of sin and was allowed to enter the afterlife. A beast called the devourer, or eater of souls, was on hand to consume the pharaoh's soul should his heart weigh more than the feather of truth.

The Egyptians used the heart in this symbolic ceremony because they realized it was a very special organ of the human body. Through their practice of embalming and mummification, they gained a great knowledge of human anatomy. This knowledge enabled them to practice medicine at a very high level and gave ancient Egyptian doctors the reputation of being the best of their time.

We still use symbolized heart drawings to mean many things and have many expressions relating to the heart. Below are listed a few. Tell what each one means and add at least 5 other "heart expressions."

1. Heartbroken_____

2. Downhearted _____

3. Heartsick _____

4. Fainthearted _____

5. Heartfelt _____

6. _____

7. _____

8. _____

9. _____

10. _____

A Scarab Paperweight

Of the many charms and amulets sacred to the ancient Egyptians, the scarab was probably the most popular.

A scarab is a stone carved to resemble the scarab beetle. The scarab beetle was chosen as a sacred symbol because it lays its eggs in decaying matter in which the young beetles hatch. To the Egyptians this process signified rebirth, and as the scarab beetles were "reborn" from decay they too looked forward to a rebirth or life after death.

One of the ways Egyptians used scarabs was during mummification. After an organ was removed from the body, the remaining space was sometimes filled by a large stone scarab. Scarabs carved in semiprecious stones are still used in jewelry and as good-luck charms. You can easily make a good-luck scarab paperweight by following the directions below.

MATERIALS: round stone with a more or less flat bottom, your favorite color of spray paint, permanent black magic marker, felt and glue (optional).

Select a nice round stone.

Spray paint it a color of your choice.

After the paint has dried, use the black magic marker to add the beetle design.

Glue a piece of felt to the bottom to prevent scratching.

Good-Luck Charms

The scarab may seem like an unlikely charm to you, but ancient Egyptians would also question the power of a four-leaf clover, a popular good-luck charm of our day. Make a list of charms, past and present, of different cultures and tell what each is supposed to do for its owner. If you have a "good-luck charm," be sure to list it.

1. _____

_____

2. _____

_____

3. _____

_____

4. _____

_____

5. _____

_____

6. _____

_____

7. _____

_____

8. _____

_____

9. _____

_____

10. _____

_____

Take a poll of your family. What are the good-luck charms they believe in? Create a graph to show the results of your poll.

The Great Sphinx

A sphinx is an imaginary creature that has a human head and a lion's body. The best known sphinx is the Great Sphinx located at Giza, Egypt. It is over 4,500 years old and stands near three great pyramids overlooking the Nile River. The head and body of the Great Sphinx were carved from a solid piece of rock. The paws and legs were made from stone blocks added to the body.

It is believed that the head of the Great Sphinx is that of a pharaoh named Khafre near whose pyramid it lies.

The Great Sphinx is about 240 feet in length, including the legs. It reaches to a height of about 66 feet.

To make a model of the Great Sphinx, follow the directions below.

To carve a sphinx you will need a large bar of soft soap and a knife or carving tool. As the soap is quite soft, the knife does not need to be very sharp. At any rate, be careful not to cut yourself. Newspaper or paper towels will be handy to put on your desk to catch the soap you trim away as you carve.

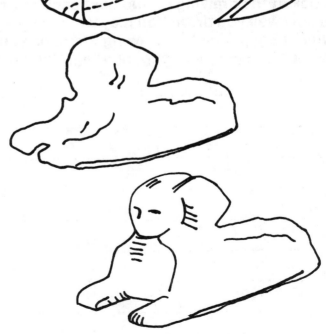

1. Begin by estimating the length of the arms and the height of the head. Then start carving.

2. After you have roughed out the head, arms and body, add the details such as the headdress and facial features.

3. Add a few finishing touches and you are finished.

VARIATION: You may wish to build a sphinx from clay instead of carving one from soap.

How to Draw Egyptian-Style

Although Egyptian art is plain and easy to understand, its style is different from the kinds of art we are used to seeing. You can imitate the Egyptian style by following a few basic rules outlined below. All you will need is a pencil, crayons and some unlined paper. When you finish compare your drawing to the ones on the next page.

1. Draw the head and neck of your figure in profile (side view). Add an eye as it would look from the front. Outline the eye in black and add a curved black eyebrow. The lips should be drawn in as viewed from the side. A black wig leaving the ear showing can be drawn for both men and women.

2. The shoulders and chest are drawn as seen from the front. The arms are drawn according to what the person is holding or doing.

3. Hips, legs and feet are drawn in profile. Men usually wore short skirts and women wore straight dresses held in place by two straps.

4. When your outline is finished, color the skin a dark tan. Clothes were usually white, but you may wish to add a brightly colored jeweled collar, which was worn by both men and women.

Look at the drawing on the next page to see how well you followed directions, not to see how well you draw. You may wish to try again. With a little practice, you will become better at Egyptian-style drawing. Perhaps your class may wish to tape all their drawings together to make one long painting. Such drawings are called frieze paintings.

How to Draw Egyptian-Style

Paper from Papyrus

Papyrus is a tall reed plant which grows well in the marshes along the Nile River in Egypt. This reed was used by the early Egyptians for making baskets, mats, boats, pens and paper. To make paper, the workman first gathered the papyrus reeds and tied them into bundles. In his workshop he chopped the reeds into smaller pieces. The size of the pieces determined the size of the paper.

The outer covering was then carefully peeled away.

The remaining center of pith was sliced into very, very thin slices.

The layers of pith were carefully placed crosswise.

A cloth was placed over the layers and the slices were beaten with a mallet.

The paper was finished with a polishing stone. This made the paper smooth.

Ink made from soot and a pen from a sharpened reed were used for writing.

How to Make Recycled Paper

1. Tear several sheets of newspaper into small pieces. Soak overnight in a large bowl with enough water to cover paper.

2. Beat the mixture until it looks "creamy." Add two cupsful of water in which three tablespoons of cornstarch have been dissolved.

3. Use a small piece of window screen and dip into the mixture to get an even layer of wood fibers coating the screen.

4. Put the coated screen on several layers of newspapers to drain. Cover with wax paper or plastic. Use brick as weight to press water from the fibers.

5. Allow recycled paper to dry overnight. Remove brick and wax paper. Peel paper off the screen.

Symbols, Then and Now

The ancient Egyptians used many symbols just as we do today. Symbols are drawings which have meanings that are instantly recognized. Every ancient Egyptian boy and girl could recognize the symbols below as they were very common and were popular for thousands of years. Study the symbols below; then turn to the next page to see some symbols that are common today.

Crook and Flail Symbols of Authority	**Shen** Symbol of Infinity	**Djed Column** Symbol of Osiris' Backbone
Udjat Protective Eye Symbol	**Lotus** Symbol of Rebirth	**Scarab** Symbol of Renewed Life
Knot of Isis Symbol of Fertility	**Ankh** Symbol of Life	**Raised Arms** Symbol of Ka, the Soul

Symbols, Then and Now

We still use symbols to suggest certain meanings just as the ancient Egyptians did. Our symbols are of course very different from theirs, and they tend to go out of style very quickly compared to those of ancient Egypt. Below are some modern symbols. See how many of them you can recognize; see how many you can add.

Logos are symbols which large corporations use for identification and advertising purposes. They are usually referred to as trademarks and are protected by copyright laws. Look through a magazine or newspaper for some easily identifiable logos. Bring them to class to find out how many your classmates can recognize.

Egyptian Gods and Goddesses

Use the descriptions on this page to identify the drawings of some of the many Egyptian gods and goddesses depicted on the next page. Indicate your answers with a letter.

_____ 1.   Thoth   _____ 5.   Horus
_____ 2.   Isis   _____ 6.   Sekhmet
_____ 3.   Osiris   _____ 7.   Hathor
_____ 4.   Anubis

1. Thoth was the god of wisdom and scribes. He had the head of an ibis, a bird similar to that of a herod except that its bill curved downward. He carried writing tools.
2. Isis was the wife of the god Osiris and mother of the god Horus. She was also the protectress of children. Her symbol was the throne. Look for it on the drawing of Isis.
3. Osiris was the god and ruler of the dead. He is wrapped as a mummy. He was thought to be the first Egyptian to be mummified. It was to his kingdom dead Egyptians wished to go.
4. Anubis was god of embalmers and of the dead. It was he who was supposed to have mummified Osiris. He was also guardian of tombs and pyramids. He had the head of a jackal.
5. Horus was the son of Osiris and Isis. He was the king of gods and the god of light and heaven. On earth he was said to live in the person of the pharaoh. He had the head of a falcon and carried an ankh in his right hand. The ankh symbolized life.
6. Sekhmet was the Egyptian goddess of war. She had the head of a lion.
7. Hathor was the cow-headed goddess of love, joy, women, childbirth and music. The Egyptians believed that when a child was born seven Hathors came to his bedside to decide his future.

Ancient Egyptians had many gods and a complex religion. You may wish to read about some of their other gods and goddesses and tell why they were worshipped.

Use encyclopedias or books on Greek and Roman mythology to research the Roman and Greek counterparts for the Egyptian god or goddess of war, death and love.

GOD OR GODDESS OF	EGYPTIAN	ROMAN	GREEK
WAR	Sekhmet		
DEATH	Osiris		
LOVE	Hathor		

Egyptian Gods and Goddesses

A

B

C

D

E

F

G

Ancient Egyptian Tourist Attractions

Study the map of ancient Egypt on the next page. Inside the circles that connect to the various spots on the map, draw key pictures similar to the ones below on the left that indicate important features of those areas. In the blocks below tell why these places were attractions for tourists, then and now.

	Memphis	
	Tell-el-Amarna	
	Red Sea	
	Giza	
	Abydos	
	Thebes	
	Mediterranean Sea	
	Valley of the Kings	
	Rosetta	
	Nile River	
	Delta	

Ancient Egyptian Tourist Attractions

ROSETTA

MEDITERRANEAN SEA

DELTA

GIZA

MEMPHIS

TELL-EL-AMARNA

NILE

RED SEA

ABYDOS

THEBES

VALLEY OF THE KINGS

Egypt Today

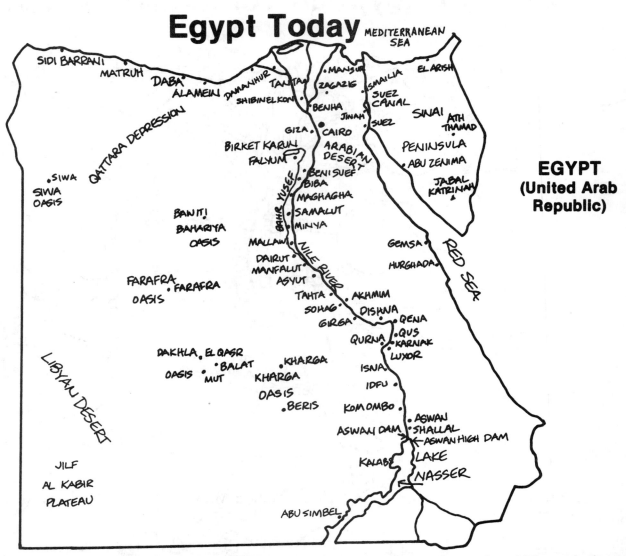

Egypt today is very different than it was during the time of the pharaohs. Although the Nile River is still the lifeblood of Egypt, its floodwaters are regulated by the High Dam at Aswan. The completion of this dam in 1971 threatened to flood the ancient city of Abu Simbel with its temples of Ramses II and Queen Nefertari beneath the waters of the newly formed Lake Nasser. An international team of engineers removed the temples piece by piece and reconstructed the monuments on higher ground.

The ancient Egyptian gods and goddesses are just memories. Most modern Egyptians are of the Islam faith. They are called Muslims. Muslims believe in one God, whom they call Allah. About ten percent modern Egyptians are Christians. They are the descendants of the ancient Egyptians, and they continue to speak a variation of the ancient Egyptian tongue. They are called Coptic Christians.

The Egyptian government today is headed by a president and a People's Assembly. A Council of Ministers advises the president. In Egyptian courts there are no juries; judges make all legal decisions.

QUESTIONS:

1. Underline Aswan High Dam and Lake Nasser on the map of modern Egypt. What monuments did the building of this dam threaten?
2. The modern capital of Egypt is Cairo. Find Cairo on the map and put a * next to it.
3. Locate the Suez Canal. What two seas are linked by it?
4. Research the Aswan High Dam and the Suez Canal in an encyclopedia. Tell how they helped modernize the ancient country of Egypt.
5. Contrast the religion and government of ancient Egypt to that of today.

24

Egyptian Symbols for Numbers

Symbol	Name of Symbol	Hindu-Arabic Symbol
/	Tally	1
∩	Heel Bone	10
⌒	Coil of Rope	100
⟼	Lotus Flower	1,000
⌐	Bent Stick	10,000
⋜	Fish	100,000
☆	Astonished Man	1,000,000

The Egyptians wrote their numbers in an ascending order, thus ones are written on the left, then tens, hundreds, thousands, etc. Six hundred and forty-one would be written by putting a one, four heel bones and six coils of rope in that order.

Translate the following Egyptian symbols into numbers.

a. |||∩∩   b. ⌒⌐   c. ⌒⌒⌒   d. |∩⌒   e. ⋜☆

Try writing the following numbers Egyptian-style.

a. 501   b. 30   c. 10   d. 2,000,000   e. 1,100

Do you think you could add or subtract using Egyptian numbers without first translating the numbers into their Hindu-Arabic symbols? Can you multiply or divide in Egyptian symbols?

Paddle Dolls

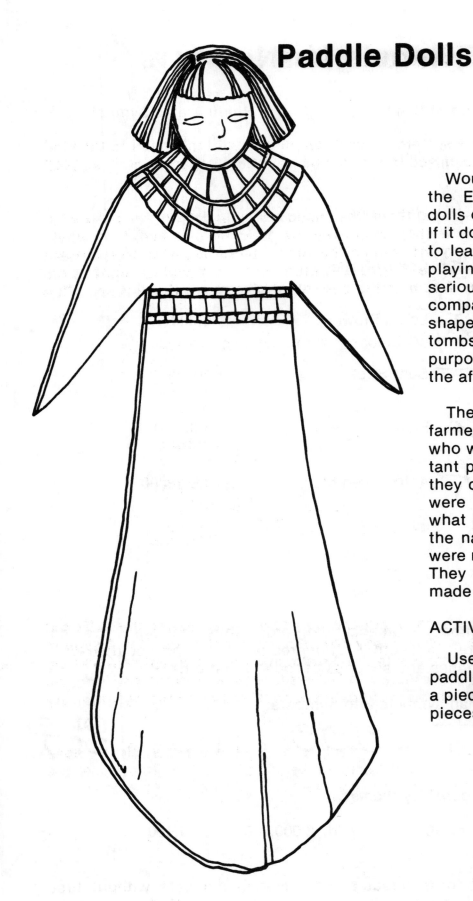

Would it surprise you to learn that the Egyptians made paddle-shaped dolls over three thousand years ago? If it does, you may be more surprised to learn that their dolls were not for playing. Paddle dolls were for a more serious purpose; they were made as company for the dead. These odd-shaped dolls were buried in the tombs of pharaohs and nobles for the purpose of serving their masters in the afterlife.

The dolls were painted to look like farmers, bakers, potters and others who would serve and work for important people in their new life. So that they could not run away, these dolls were designed without feet, somewhat in the shape of paddles, hence the name paddle dolls. Paddle dolls were made from thin pieces of wood. They were carved and painted. Hair made of strings of beads was added.

ACTIVITY:

Use the outline to the left to make a paddle doll. Cut it out and glue it onto a piece of cardboard. Color it. Attach pieces of black yarn for hair.

Hieroglyphs

Hieroglyphs (hy-er-oh-glifs) is a system of Egyptian picture writing similar to the kind the American Indian used. It is believed that this kind of writing began as early as 3000 B.C.

When early Egpytians began writing them, they used a simple drawing to show what they meant. For example, if they wished to convey the meaning of a bee, they would draw a bee. This is called an ideogram. In time the simple pictures began to represent words or syllables which sounded like the drawn picture, but the meaning might be entirely different. For example, the figure of the bee might also mean the verb, *be.* This type of writing is known as syllabic.

Tell what these pictures may mean in ideograms and syllabic writing:

The final stage in hieroglyphs was using the symbols to represent the different sounds of the Egyptian language in the way that our alphabet does. The Egyptian alphabet consists of twenty-five symbols. In the development of the Egyptian alphabet, the ideograph and syllabic forms continued to be used, making a combination of all three forms. This combination made the writing and understanding of hieroglyphs very difficult.

In writing, the ancient Egyptians did not normally write out vowels; they simply used the consonants. In other words, the word *horse* would simply be *hrs*. To be sure the reader got the word right, sometimes an ideogram would be added after the word.

hrs

Hieroglyphs

If all this sounds complicated to you, take heart; it was for them also. So much so that few people learned to read and write in ancient Egyptian times, and it took many years to become a trained writer of the language. The people who mastered the reading and writing of hieroglyphs were called scribes. The scribes of ancient Egypt were greatly admired and respected for their ability, knowledge and artistic skills. Becoming a scribe was one of the few ways in ancient Egypt that a person of the lower classes was able to rise above his station in life.

QUESTIONS and ACTIVITIES:

1. Draw an ideograph for the words *seal* and *meat*.

2. What might your drawings in question 1 mean in syllabic forms?

    _____

    _____

3. Try writing a sentence by using only the consonants in those words. See if a classmate can understand the meaning of the sentence you have written.

    _____

    _____

4. Do you think there are advantages of using ideographs instead of an alphabet? Why or why not? _____

    _____

    _____

5. Discuss the advantages of an alphabet over ideographs. _____

    _____

    _____

6. Use the hieroglythic alphabet on the next page to write your name and a message to a friend.

7. Design some ideographs of your own and write a message in your ideographs. Give it to a classmate. Note whether or not it was interpreted as you intended.

Hieroglyphs

HIEROGLYPH	SOUND	HIEROGLYPH	SOUND	HIEROGLYPH	SOUND
Vulture	a (ah)	Owl	M	Pool	sh
Reed leaf	i as in fill	Water	n	Hill	q
Two leafs	ee (ēe) or y	Mouth	r	Basket	k or c
Hand and arm	a as in car	Shelter	h	Stand	g
Quail	w or v	twisted flax	h said quickly as in ha!	Loaf	t
Foot	b	hole	kh	Rein	th
Mat	p	Udder or tail	ch or sh	Hand	d
Horned snake	f	Folded cloth	s or z	Cobra	j or dj
Lion	l				

The Rosetta Stone

In July 1799, Napoleon's army was making fortifications in northern Egypt after conquering the country. One of the French soldiers who was digging in the area near Rosetta hit upon a small black rock. Into the rock were carved three different styles of writing. It was soon realized that two of the writing styles were of ancient Egyptian. Both of the Egyptian styles were so ancient that no one had been able to translate them for many centuries. The third language was Greek and easily translatable by scholars. When the scholars realized that the message was probably the same one written in three different ways, the knowledge of Greek was used to give clues to the meaning of the hieroglyphs.

Suppose you are an archeologist and have discovered some ancient writings carved in stone. The first clue to the meaning of the words comes to you when you realize that the message is written in two different languages, one of which you can read. From this clue can you decode some of the words below? All of the words are about ancient Egypt.

T U T A N K H A M E N

1.
2.
3.
4.
5.
6.

Curse or Coincidence?

The greatest Egyptian archeological discovery, the tomb of Tutankhamen, was due largely to the work of an Englishman named Howard Carter. Howard Carter fell in love with Egypt when he was only eighteen years old. The five-thousand-year-old pyramids, the Nile River and the cloudless blue sky fascinated him; but, most of all, Howard Carter was drawn to Egypt by the tombs carved out of rock in the Valley of the Kings near the ancient city of Thebes, now Luxor.

It was in 1891 that Carter, who lacked a college education, trained himself to read hieroglyphs, the ancient Egyptian language. His hard work and enthusiasm so impressed Professor Percy Newman, an Egyptologist, that he asked Carter to accompany him on his next trip to Egypt.

Possessed with great energy, Carter learned quickly and soon rose in the ranks as an official and scholar in the Egyptian Department of Antiquities. His main concern became the preservation and guarding of the tombs of ancient pharaohs from grave robbers and wealthy art collectors. In his work Carter soon learned every foot of the Valley of the Kings.

In 1902 a wealthy amateur Egyptologist, Theodore Davis, came to Egypt. Carter was assigned to help him. Davis was hoping to find an unrobbed tomb. For twelve years Howard Carter helped with the digging. In that period of time they never discovered an unrobbed tomb although they were successful in finding other important objects.

In 1914 Davis believed that he had discovered all that was left in the 5,000 years of the Valley of the Kings, and in the same year Lord Carnarvon, a wealthy Englishman, with Carter's help began searching for an unrobbed tomb. For seven years Carter and Carnarvon found almost nothing. It was now 1922 and Lord Carnarvon was ready to give up. Howard Carter knew of one small patch of ground as yet unexplored and convinced Carnarvon to make one last dig. On this last try Carter hit upon a set of steps. At the bottom of the steps was the three-thousand-year-old unbroken seal placed on the tomb of Tutankhamen by his Egyptian priests.

Curse or Coincidence?

After the tomb of Tutankhamen was opened and his mummy examined, many people objected and felt that the tomb should have remained undisturbed. Some people went so far as to call the archeologists themselves grave robbers. Newspapers around the world began to run articles about the "pharaoh's curse." These rumors were further fueled when Lord Carnarvon died of a mosquito bite only two months after the discovery. Two strange coincidences at the time of his death brought more publicity. When Carnarvon was staying in a hotel in Cairo, Egypt, all the lights in the city went out without explanation moments before his death, and at the very moment of his death, his dog died. A short time later another archeologist who helped open the tomb died in the same hotel. A friend of Carnarvon's died a day after visiting the tomb, and another friend died shortly after viewing the tomb. The doctor who x-rayed Tutankhamen's mummy died in 1924. All in all by 1929, six years after the tomb had been opened, twenty-two people who had in some way been involved had died. This number includes Carnarvon's wife who also died of an insect bite. Carnarvon's secretary, Richard Bethell, died in 1929 after collapsing on his bed. Bethell's father committed suicide on hearing the news of his son's death. In still another strange incident, a small boy was killed by the hearse of Bethell's father on the way to the cemetery. With each death the publicity heightened. The greatest fact to dispel the "curse" was that Howard Carter himself lived to be sixty-six.

1. Do you think that publicity such as the "pharaoh's curse" can "talk" people into dying?

2. What are some sensational issues that newspapers are writing about at the present time?

3. Can you think of another so called "curse" that has received wide public attention through the newspapers or other media?

4. Why do newspapers and other media such as television dwell on sensational stories like the "pharaoh's curse?"

5. To learn more about some ancient Egyptians who left their mark on history, research one of the following:

Menes   Ramses II   Imhotep   Akhenaton (Akhenaten)   Hatshepsut

The Plan of Tutankhamen's Tomb

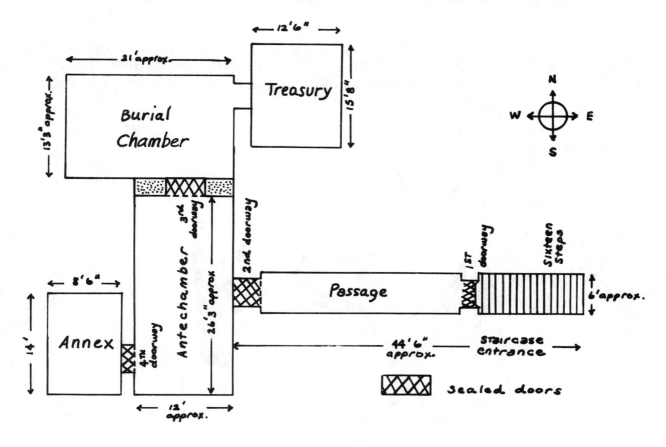

Study the above drawing to answer the questions below concerning the plan of King Tutankhamen's tomb.

1. How many steps led to the passageway? _____

2. How many sealed doorways were there in the entire tomb? _____

3. What was the name of the room beyond the second door? _____

4. In which direction from the antechamber did the burial chamber lie? _____

5. What was the largest room of the tomb?_____

6. What room was located east of the burial chamber? _____

33

You Are the Archeologist

Archeologists often work with clues. Suppose you are an archeologist digging in the Valley of the Kings. A box containing the items pictured below has just been found. After you have examined them, how would you answer the following questions?

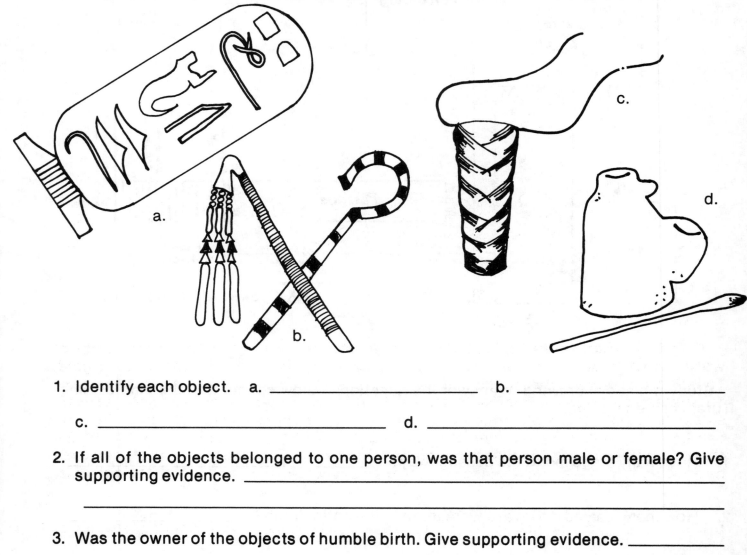

1. Identify each object. a. _____ b. _____

   c. _____ d. _____

2. If all of the objects belonged to one person, was that person male or female? Give supporting evidence. _____
   _____

3. Was the owner of the objects of humble birth. Give supporting evidence. _____
   _____
   _____

4. What title might that person have had? _____

ACTIVITY:
Prepare a bag of five to ten objects which, if found five thousand years from today, would tell something of your existence—your likes, dislikes, interests, possible occupation, etc. Have a class exchange of bags. Try to identify class members from their clues.

34

A Series of Boxes

King Tutankhamen was buried inside three coffins. The two outer coffins were of wood plated in gold. The innermost coffin which held his mummy was of solid gold. These coffins were body-shaped and are known as anthropoid coffins. As in the case of Tutankhamen, it was the custom in ancient Egypt to place the mummies of pharaohs inside a series of coffins decorated with portraits of the person as he looked in life. You can easily learn to make a series of boxes which will fit one inside the other as the anthropoid coffins did by following the instructions below. Decorate the tops of the boxes by drawing Egyptian-style drawings on the tops and writing hieroglyphs on the bottoms.

MATERIALS: white or gold-colored construction paper, scissors, colored pencils or crayons.

PROCEDURE: To make the three boxes and their tops you will first need to cut the paper you are using into six squares: an 8-inch square for the bottom and an 8½-inch square for the top of the largest box, a 6 and 6½-inch square for the medium box and a 4 and 4½-inch square for the smallest box. Decorate the outside of the 8½, 6½ and 4½-inch squares with Egyptian-style portraits, and the 8, 6, and 4-inch bottom squares with hieroglyphs. The instructions on the next page will show you how to make the squares into boxes.

A Series of Boxes

1. Begin with an 8-inch square piece of paper.

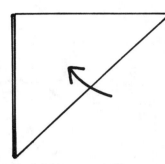

2. Fold it once diagonally and crease the edge.

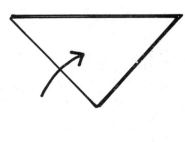

3. Fold diagonally again and crease the edge.

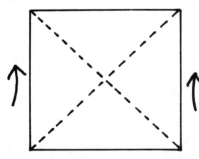

4. Open paper to the original size.

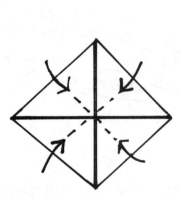

5. Turn in all four corners to meet in center and crease.

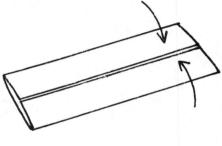

6. Turn in two opposite sides to meet in center and crease. Turn in the other two opposite sides and crease making a small square.

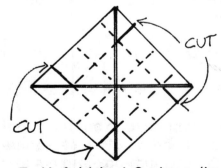

7. Unfold last 2 steps (to step 5). Make cuts on creases as shown by heavy lines.

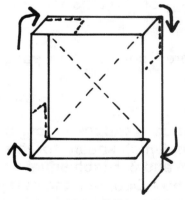

8. Bend the cut piece inside the flap of the opposite edge. Repeat at the other three corners.

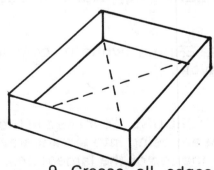

9. Crease all edges. To make a top, repeat all steps using an 8½-inch square. To make a series of boxes, repeat all steps using 6, 6½, 4, 4½-inch squares of paper.

Make Your Own Hieroglyphic Code Wheel

The ancient Egyptians sometimes used codes in tombs to confuse would-be grave robbers. By designing your own hieroglyphic alphabet, you and a friend can use a code wheel for sending and translating messages quickly. Below are instructions for making a simple code wheel designed by Leon Alberti over 400 years ago.

1. Begin by pasting the two circles on page 42 onto a stiff piece of cardboard.

2. Neatly cut out the circles.

3. With your partner design a symbol for each letter of the alphabet.

4. Starting with the letter A, draw your symbols in the spaces on the smaller circle. Design a symbol for each letter of the alphabet and keep the symbols in order. You and your partner must have the same symbols for each letter in order to translate messages.

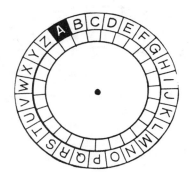

5. Place the smaller circle over the larger one and attach with a paper fastener or tack onto a soft wooden base with a thumbtack.

6. Turn the wheel until the symbol you and your partner have chosen to represent the letter A is in place. You are now operating in that key. For example, if you use the symbol # to represent A, it should be under A and # is your key.

7. Use a paper clip to hold the wheel in place when you are decoding. Change keys whenever you wish. Change symbols whenever someone has cracked your key and your messages are no longer secret.

Make Your Own Hieroglyphic Code Wheel

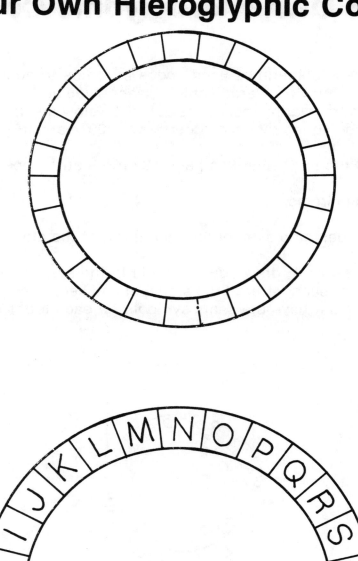

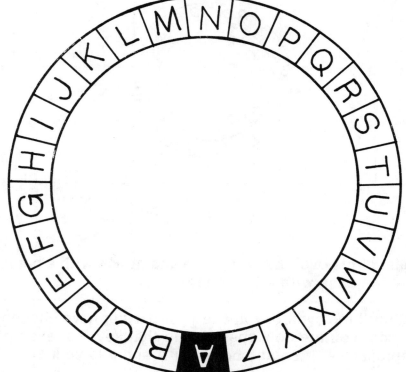

Paper-Cut Clues

You will enjoy using paper-cut clues in your study of ancient Egypt. Begin by placing the pattern below over a sheet of construction paper. Place a thick newspaper under both. Use an X-acto knife or a single-edged razor blade to cut along all lines. Place the cut construction paper over a mystery picture or drawing such as the one on page 44. Open windows until you can determine the picture underneath. The numbers of open windows is the score, and low score wins. Use the paper-cut clues on other pictures from magazines, textbooks or have students draw pictures that relate to Egypt to use on their classmates.

Nefertiti

The statue of Nefertiti's head, which was found in ancient Egyptian ruins, is well-known throughout the world. Nefertiti is famous for her beauty and for the fact that she was the mother-in-law of Tutankhamen. She was the wife of a pharaoh called Amenhotep IV. Amenhotep IV changed his name to Akhenaten in honor of the sun god, Aten. Akhenaten and Nefertiti had six daughters. Their eldest daughter, Meritaten married a man called Smenkhkare. Their second daughter, Meketaten, died in infancy. The third daughter, Ankhesenamen, was the wife of Tutankhamen. Amenhotep IV and his eldest son-in-law, Smenkhkare, died at about the same time. Since women were not allowed to rule, Tutankhamen became the next pharaoh. His reign, however, was short. It is believed that Tutankhamen was about nineteen when he died. Little is known about the three youngest daughters of Nefertiti and Amenhotep IV. After the death of Tutankhamen, the throne of Egypt fell into the hands of a nobleman. The fate of Tutankhamen's wife, Ankhesenamen, is also uncertain. The family tree on the next page will help you to understand the relationship of this famous ancient Egyptian family.

A Family Tree of Egyptian Royalty

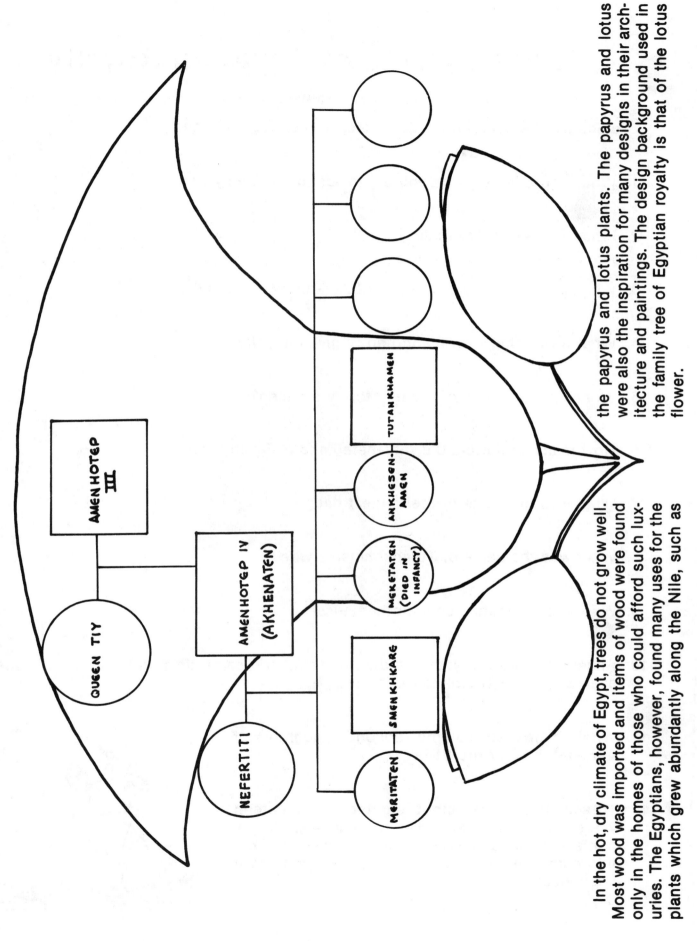

Queen Tiy — **Amenhotep III**

Nefertiti — **Amenhotep IV (Akhenaten)**

Meritaten — **Smenkhkare**

Meketaten (died in infancy)

Ankhesen-Amen — **Tutankhamen**

In the hot, dry climate of Egypt, trees do not grow well. Most wood was imported and items of wood were found only in the homes of those who could afford such luxuries. The Egyptians, however, found many uses for the plants which grew abundantly along the Nile, such as the papyrus and lotus plants. The papyrus and lotus were also the inspiration for many designs in their architecture and paintings. The design background used in the family tree of Egyptian royalty is that of the lotus flower.

A Family Tree of Egyptian Royalty

To answer the questions below, refer to the preceding page.

1. What figure is used to denote females in the family tree?

2. What figure denotes males?

3. What was the name of the son of Amenhotep III and Queen Tiy?

4. What new name did Amenhotep IV give himself?

5. What was the name of Amenhotep IV's queen?

6. How many daughters did Akhenaten and Nefertiti have?

7. What was the name of their eldest daughter?

8. What was the name of Tutankhamen's wife?

9. Who was Tutankhamen's mother-in-law?

10. Akhenaten and Smenkhkare died at about the same time. What effect did these events have on Tutankhamen's life?

11. What happened to the second daughter of Akhenaten and Nefertiti?

12. Tutankhamen was about eighteen or nineteen years old when he died. He was succeeded by a noble servant named Ay. No one really knows how this came about. What do you think might have happened?

Senet

Although ancient Egyptians did not enjoy the wide variety of games that we do today, they spent many hours playing a game similar to our game of checkers. Their game was called Senet. A simplified version of Senet is given below.

This version of Senet is a game for two players to be played on a board of twenty-five squares. The object of the game is to take as many of your opponent's pieces, called kelbs, as possible. To do this, you must have two kelbs, one on each side of your opponent's kelb. Kelbs can be moved up, down or sideways, but not diagonally. Kelbs can only move one space at a time, and they can't "jump" other kelbs.

MATERIALS: Board of twenty-five squares, twenty-four kelbs, twelve each of two different colors. Checkers or buttons can be used for kelbs.

Rules for Simplified Senet

1. Toss a coin or roll a die to decide who goes first.

2. First player puts two kelbs on the squares called oyoons.

3. Second player does the same. No kelbs are placed on the center square.

4. Continue to alternate, placing kelbs on the board until all the kelbs are on the board.

Step 2

Step 3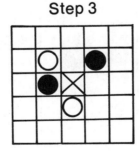

Steps 4 & 5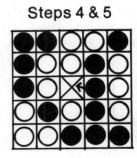

5. First player moves one kelb into the center square. A player who cannot move on the first round passes.

Senet

6. Kelbs are taken only when they are trapped between two of the opponent's kelbs after the game has begun. If a player willfully puts his kelb between two of his opponent's, he cannot be captured.

7. Each time a player captures a kelb, he is entitled to another move. Multiple captures (capturing two kelbs with one move) entitle capturer to only one move.

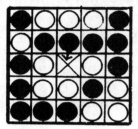

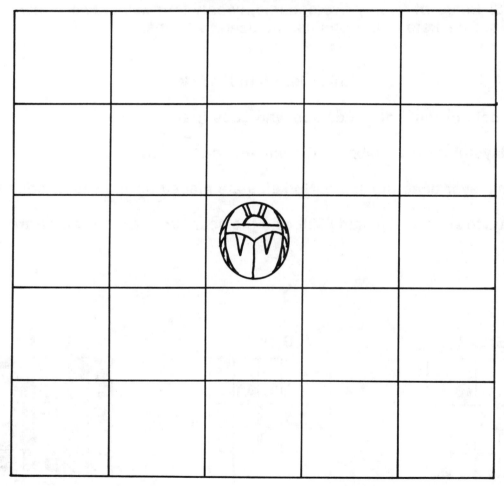

8. When a player captures an opponent's kelb, he must pick up the kelb.

9. Winner is the one who captures the most kelbs or whose opponent cannot move or refuses to move.

10. This version of Senet can be played very quickly. Tournaments should be set up for winners to play winners and losers to play losers to determine the grand champion.

Games People Play

Think of the many kinds of games you have played in your life. You have probably played most of the types listed below. Tell what is meant by each type and give at least one example of each.

Childhood games

Board games

Card games

Party games

Pencil and paper games

Devise an original game of any of the above types.

Make a set of rules and playing instructions for your game.

If your game requires parts to play, make the parts you will need.

Design a package or box to house your game.

Write an advertisement, or make an audio or videotape commercial for selling your game.

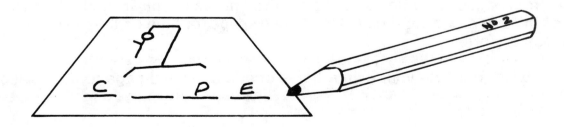

Cleopatra

Cleopatra was the most famous of all Egyptian queens. She was a descendant of the Ptolemies, a Greek family that ruled Egypt for over three hundred years. Her father at the time of his death left the throne to Cleopatra and her brother. Shortly thereafter her brother had Cleopatra exiled so that he could become the sole ruler of Egypt.

When Julius Caesar came to Egypt, Cleopatra devised a scheme for getting into his palace to ask for aid against her brother. She had herself rolled up into a rug. The rug was sent to Caesar as a gift. When the servants unrolled the rug, the beautiful Cleopatra emerged. Caesar was soon captivated by Cleopatra and helped her regain the throne to share this time with a younger brother. When Caesar returned to Rome she followed him and lived there until the time of his death. She then returned to Egypt with her young son. Not long after her return her younger brother with whom she shared the throne died. Many believe that Cleopatra had him poisoned so that she and her son could become the new rulers.

At about the same time the Roman Empire, without Caesar's leadership, began to crumble. It was divided, and Mark Antony, a friend of Caesar's, was given the Eastern Empire to rule. To keep Egypt from becoming a province of Rome, Cleopatra went to Mark Antony for help. Antony also fell under her charm and agreed to her request. He not only allowed Egypt to remain an independent country, he planned to make himself the sole ruler of the Roman Empire with Cleopatra as his queen. Because of his great love for Cleopatra, whom the Romans did not trust, Antony lost power and support in Rome. As soon as Cleopatra realized that Antony would never become ruler of Rome, she sent him a message saying that by the time he received her note she would be dead. Of course she lied, but Antony believed the message and committed suicide. Just before he died, he learned the truth and asked to be carried to Cleopatra, where he died in her arms.

Cleopatra now tried to bring Octavian, the ruler of Rome, under her spell, but she was not successful. Rather than live as a prisoner of Rome, she committed suicide by allowing herself to be bitten on the arm by a poisonous snake called an asp. After her death, Octavian decreed that her body be buried next to Mark Antony's. He also decreed that her young son be executed so that he might not make any claim to the throne of Rome.

If newspapers existed at the time of Cleopatra, there is no doubt that she would have made the front pages many times during her lifetime, as people in ancient times were as interested in news as we are today. Use the newspaper outline on the next page to finish the suggested stories.

You may wish to create your own articles or add a second page to the newspaper.

The Giza Gazette

VOLUME 1　　　　　　　　　　　　　　　　　　　ISSUE 1

No Nile overflow due to drought

Scribes strike!

Crackdown on tomb robbers

Pyramid litter results in ban on traffic

Dear Neffi:
What's wrong with today's kids?

Obituaries: Cleopatra Ptolemy

Women Who Have Ruled

Cleopatra was one of many women in history who ruled or headed the government of a country. Listed below are other women who left their marks on the pages of history. Can you tell when and how each of these women earned her fame?

1. Elizabeth I of England _____

_____

_____

2. Isabella I of Spain _____

_____

_____

3. Liliuokalani of Hawaii _____

_____

_____

4. Golda Meir of Israel _____

_____

_____

5. Indira Nehru Gandhi of India _____

_____

_____

6. Margaret Thatcher of Great Britain _____

_____

_____

Can you add two more to the above list?

7. _____

_____

8. _____

_____

Famous Couples

The story of Cleopatra's romance with Mark Antony has survived for 2,000 years. There are many other famous couples who live on in history, literature and art. Match and identify as many of the couples below as you can. Tell which are real and which are fictional and how each couple earned fame.

Romeo	Isabella
Mark Antony	Victoria
Charles	Harriet
Robert	Martha
Mickey	Diana
Dante	Clementine
Napoleon	Minnie
George	Elizabeth
Albert	Eleanor
Ozzie	Juliet
Winston	Cleopatra
Dagwood	Scarlett
Rhett	Blondie
Henry II	Josephine
Ferdinand	Beatrice

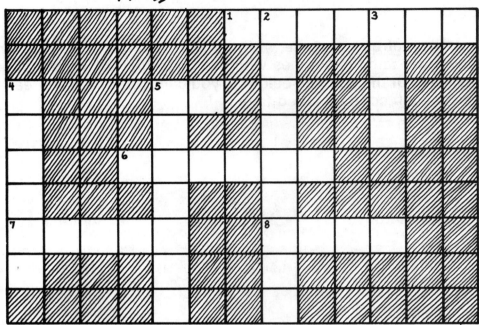

Try your hand at decoding the hieroglyphics to solve this crossword puzzle. You will need to refer to page 29 for clues as to the meanings of the hieroglyphic symbols. In places where no hierogylphic symbol exists, the English letter is used. Once the clues have been decoded, use the clues to solve the crossword.

The Three Crowns of Egypt

Before the year 3000 B.C. Egypt was two separate kingdoms. They were known as Upper and Lower Egypt.

Lower Egypt, which lay to the north, included the great city of Memphis and the Nile Delta. Upper Egypt, or the Valley as it was known, extended southward from Memphis to Aswan. Menes, an early Egyptian ruler, is given credit for uniting the two Egypts into a single country.

After unification, the Egyptian pharaohs began to wear a ceremonial crown which was a combination of the crowns of both regions. The white crown of Upper Egypt was placed on the head first. The red crown of Lower Egypt was fitted over and around the white one. The pharaoh wore the double crown to show that he was ruler of both Egypts. In wartime, the double crown was set aside and the pharaoh donned a blue one which was known as the war crown.

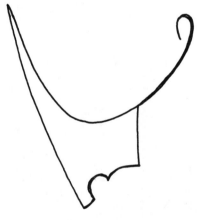
Red Crown

White Crown

Double Crown

To make the double crown of Egypt gather the materials listed below and follow the instructions on the next two pages.

| Red poster paper | scissors | ruler |
| White poster paper | stapler | pencil |

The Three Crowns of Egypt

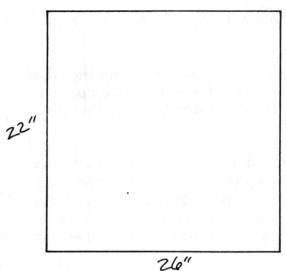

1. Cut a piece of white poster board into a 22" by 26" rectangle.

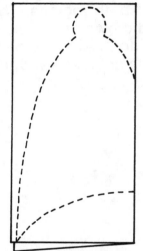

3. Draw the shape of the crown and cut out.

2. Fold along the center line

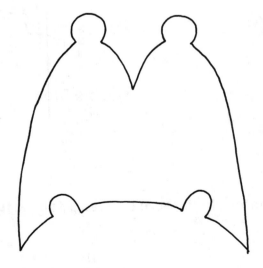

4. Fit to head and cut out openings for ears.

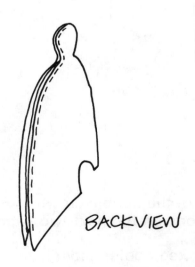

BACKVIEW

5. Trim excess, if too large, and staple.

The Three Crowns of Egypt

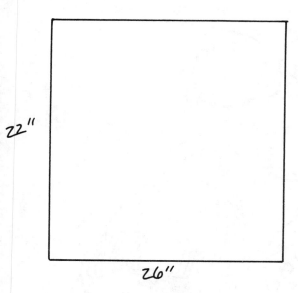

1. Cut a piece of red poster board into a 22″ by 26″ rectangle.

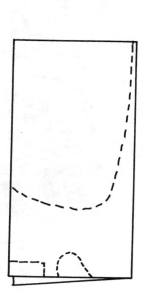

3. Draw the shape of the red crown and cut out. Fit to wear over the white crown.

FOLD

2. Fold along the center line.

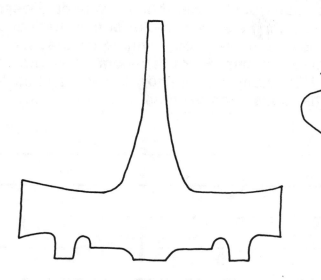

4. Make decoration and cobra. Attach decorations.

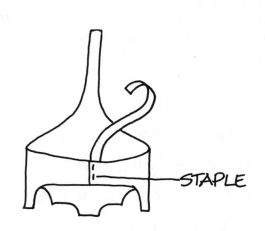

STAPLE

5. Staple at front and wear over white crown.

Hats Off to You!

Hats are worn for many reasons. The official hat of a king, a crown, is worn as a symbol of authority. A policeman's hat is a symbol of authority also, but as do most hats, it serves several purposes. The policeman's hat tells the wearer's occupation as does that of a nurse or chef. It also protects the wearer's head from the weather. Most people wear hats for protection from the elements or to guard the head from the effects of heat and cold. Whatever the reason for wearing hats may be, most people will agree they have been with us since ancient times and are likely to remain. Below are some well-known expressions which have the word *hat* in them. How many of them do you know and use? How many others can you add to the list? What does each expression really mean?

1. Hats off to you! _____

2. She wears many hats. _____

3. His head is too big for his hat. _____

4. He threw his hat into the ring. _____

5. Talking through his hat . . . _____

6. High hat! _____

On the back of this activity sheet you can list other "hat" expressions that you have heard.

An Egyptian Brunch

Ancient Egyptians did not have the great variety of foods which we enjoy today. Bread, baked in flat loaves, honey, dates, figs and grapes were among their favorites and were enjoyed by all. Roast duck and other waterfowl, fish and wild game, such as gazelles and desert hares, supplied protein to their diets. A wide variety of vegetables, such as cucumbers, onions, peas, beans and young papyrus stalks, were also eaten. Wine and beer were common beverages. Sometimes domestic animals were force-fed to make them fat and tender before they were served at a gourmet's table.

You can prepare a simple brunch for your class to enjoy while studying Egypt by gathering the following foods: homemade bread, grape juice, honey, grapes, figs and dates. Such a menu would please any ancient Egyptian for breakfast or lunch.

To make your brunch more interesting, prepare a large poster of the hieroglyphic alphabet and post it in the classroom. Use the hieroglyphic alphabet to write out place cards for everyone in the class. Put the place cards on desks other than the usual classroom seating arrangement. Have students find their brunch seat by decoding the place cards with the help of the poster.

Petesuchos, the Sacred Crocodile

The Egyptian god Sobek was often symbolized by a crocodile named Petesuchos. The ancient Egyptians believed that the body of Petesuchos contained the soul of Sobek, and in his honor they named a city Crocodilopolis. Crocodiles were in fact held in such high esteem by the ancient Egyptians that they were often adorned with precious jewels and kept as pets in pools. After death they were sometimes mummified and buried in special crocodile cemeteries.

Ancient Egyptians made models of crocodiles to place in tombs and as toys for children. Follow the instructions below to make a modern crocodile model.

MATERIALS: Soft "tin" can, strong scissors, nail, hammer.

PROCEDURE: Follow the steps below.

1. Remove top and bottom ends of the can.

2. Cut the can open with the scissors and carefully press flat.

3. Use the pattern on the next page or create a creature of your own design. Use the hammer and nail to make the eyes, nose, etc.

4. Cut out the crocodile shape. Bend the legs and head to get a natural look.

VARIATION: Petesuchos can also be made from the same pattern using construction paper.

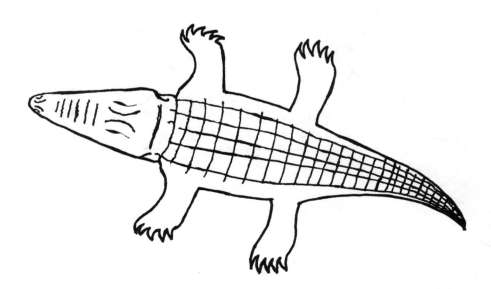

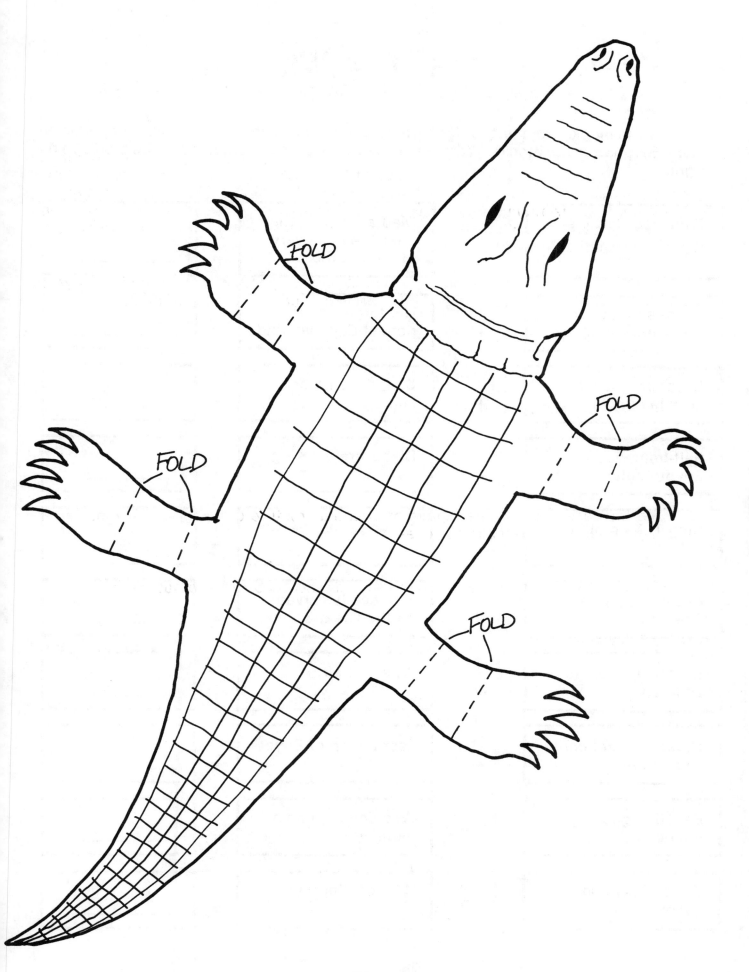

FOLD

FOLD

FOLD

FOLD

1 + 1 = Who

Read the blocks from left to right. There are two hints to the identity of a famous ancient Egyptian in the blocks. Write the name of the person described in the block on the right.

Financed Carter's work	+	Died a few months after the discovery of Tut's tomb	= _____
Egyptian pharaoh who died young	+	His tomb was the richest Egyptian find	= _____
Egyptian god who slew his uncle	+	Son of Osiris and Isis	= _____
Self-trained Egyptologist	+	Discoverer of King Tut's tomb	= _____
King Tut's mother-in-law	+	Noted for her beauty	= _____
Ancient Egyptian Pharaoh	+	His face is carved on the Great Sphinx	= _____
Egyptian goddess of children	+	Wife of Osiris	= _____
Noted for her beauty and charm	+	Last queen of Egypt	= _____
Egyptian god of the dead	+	Was depicted as a mummy	= _____
Young Egyptian queen	+	Wife of King Tut	= _____

Please use this revised Answer Key in place of the one on pages 59 and 60 at the end of the book.

Answer Key

Page 3
1. Lakes Albert, Edward and Victoria
2. Khartoum
3. Khartoum and Cairo
4. Six cataracats

Page 5
2. Hanging Gardens of Babylon. Built by Nebuchadnezzar in the sixth century B.C.
3. Statue of Zeus in Greece. Built about 500 B.C.
4. Temple of Diana in Asia Minor. Built about 350 B.C.
5. Mausoleum at Halicarnassus in Asia Minor. It was built about 350 B.C. We get the word mausoleum from this tomb.
6. The Colossus of Rhodes. This is a statue of the god Apollo. It was built about 280 B.C.
7. The Lighthouse of Alexandria. Build around 250 B.C.

Page 19
Top row left to right: I love Atlanta, Railroad crossing, Star of David.
Second row: Santa Claus, Smiley face, Stoplight.
Third row: Handicapped, Cross of Christianity, American flag.
Fourth row: Checkered flag (end of a race), Hospital, Handshake (friendship)

Page 20
1. C, 2. E, 3. F, 4. B, 5. G, 6. A, 7. D.

GOD OF	EGYPTIAN	ROMAN	GREEK
WAR	Sekhmet	Mars	Ares
DEATH	Osiris	Orcus/Dis	Pluto/Hades
LOVE	Hathor	Venus	Aphrodite

Page 22
Memphis—The Step Pyramid is located near Memphis. It was also the old capital of Egypt.
Tell-el-Amarna—Akhenaten's capital. Akhenaten was considered a heretic as he believed in only one god, Aten, the sun.
Red Sea—Egyptian ships traveled on the Red Sea to parts of Africa.
Giza—Location of the Great Sphinx and three great pyramids.
Abydos—City known for the worshipping of the god Osiris.
Thebes—The great temple of Karnak is located in this once capital city.
Mediterranean Sea—Trading ships to and from Egypt used this great body of water.
Valley of the Kings—King Tut's tomb is located here, as well as other pharaohs.
Rosetta—Place where the Rosetta stone was found. It became the key for deciphering hieroglyphs.
Nile River—The Nile River was to ancient Egyptians as a super highway is to us.
Delta—Fertile delta of the Nile River.

Page 24
1. Temples of Ramses II and Queen Nefertari
3. Mediterranean Sea and the Red Sea
4. Answers will vary.
5. The ancient Egyptians had many gods and goddesses and the pharaoh was the absolute ruler. Today most Egyptians believe in one God; their government is headed by a president and a People's Assembly.

Page 25
a. 23 b. 10,100, c. 300 d. 111 e. 1,200,000

Page 28
1. Drawing of a seal (animal). *Seal* can also be a verb as to seal a document in syllabic writing. The drawing of a piece of meat can mean the verb *to meet* in syllabic writing.

Page 30
1. Ka
2. Mummy
3. Amen-Re
4. Nile
5. Cleopatra
6. Egypt

Page 32
1 to 4 Answers will vary.
5. Menes—early pharaoh who united Upper and Lower Egypt around 3000 B.C.
Ramses II—Egyptian pharaoh noted for his bravery against the Hittites. Egypt rose to great heights during his reign.
Imhotep—Ancient Egyptian doctor and architect. He is considered to be the first physician for whom we have a name.
Akhenaton or Akhenaten—Egyptian pharaoh who reformed the ancient Egyptian religion from one of many gods to that of one god, Aten, the sun god. His reforms did not last.
Hatshepsut—Egyptian queen and the only woman to rule as a pharaoh after the death of her husband.

Page 33
1. Sixteen
2. Four
3. Antechamber
4. North
5. Antechamber
6. Treasury

Page 34
1. a. Cartouche drawn around the name of a pharaoh or queen. (A cartouche represented a rope showing that the ruler was lord of all within.)
b. Crook and flail, symbols of authority.
c. False beard of Osiris.
d. Kohl jar and brush. (Kohl was used to make up the eyes.)
2. False beard was worn only by royal males.
3. No. Crook and flail were symbols of authority of a ruler. Cartouche and false beard were also symbols of royalty.
4. Pharaoh

Page 42
1. Circles
2. Squares
3. Amenhotep IV
4. Akhenaten
5. Nefertiti
6. Six
7. Meritaten
8. Ankhesenamen
9. Nefertiti
10. He became pharaoh
11. Died in infancy
12. Answers will vary.

Page 48
1. Elizabeth I was a famous English queen. Under her reign England rose to become the greatest power of the time. Queen from 1558-1603
2. Isabella of Spain is noted for helping and encouraging Columbus. Queen from 1474-1504
3. Queen Liliuokalani is a famous Hawaiian queen. (1891-1893)
4. Golda Meir was the first woman prime minister of Israel. (1969-1974)
5. Indira Nehru Gandhi was the first woman prime minister of India. (1966-1984)
6. Margaret Thatcher is the first woman prime minister of Great Britain. (1979-   )

Page 49
Romeo and Juliet, Shakespearean play, fictional
Mark Antony and Cleopatra, historical, also famous in plays, movies, etc.
Charles and Diana, factual. Prince and Princess of Wales
Robert and Elizabeth Browning, factual. Both were English poets.
Mickey and Minnie, fictional cartoon characters
Dante and Beatrice, factual. Dante was a famous Italian poet.
Napoleon and Josephine, historical fact
George and Martha Washington, historical fact
Albert and Queen Victoria of England, historical fact
Ozzie and Harriet, fictional and fact. They were married to each other in real life. Famous television couple.
Winston Churchill and Clementine, historical fact
Dagwood and Blondie, fictional cartoon characters
Rhett Butler and Scarlett O'Hara, fictional characters in the book and movie, Gone with the Wind
Henry II and Eleanor of Aquitaine, historical. Henry II was an English king during the Middle Ages.
Ferdinand and Isabella, historical rulers of Spain

Page 50

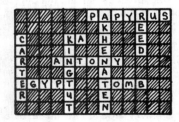

Page 60
Lord Carnarvon
Tutankhamen
Horus
Carter
Nefertiti
Khafre
Isis
Cleopatra
Osiris
Ankhesenamen